Intermediate to Advanced

DISTINCTIVE PIANO SOLOS

Arranged by Jason Lyle Black "The Backwards Piano Man®"

2   The Avengers

10   Beethoven's Fifth

5   Everybody Talks

16   The Evolution of Taylor Swift

22   Frozen Medley

27   The Hanging Tree

30   I Will Wait

36   I Won't Give Up

44   Lips Are Movin'

39   Radioactive

48   See You Again

52   Shut Up and Dance

60   Sugar

56   Thriller

ISBN 978-1-4950-3616-3

HAL•LEONARD®
CORPORATION

7777 W. BLUEMOUND RD. P.O. BOX 13819 MILWAUKEE, WI 53213

Visit Hal Leonard Online at
www.halleonard.com

THE AVENGERS
from the Motion Picture THE AVENGERS

Composed by ALAN SILVESTRI
Arranged by Jason Lyle Black

♩ = 115-120

EVERYBODY TALKS

Words and Music by TYLER GLENN
and TIM PAGNOTTA
Arranged by Jason Lyle Black

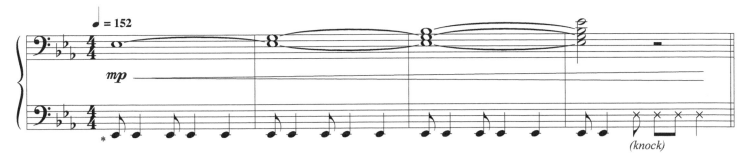

* *The L.H. throughout this piece creates a fun "accompaniment percussion."*
Be sure to keep the L.H. quiet so it doesn't detract from the R.H. melody.

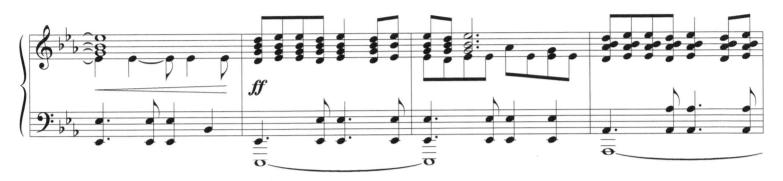

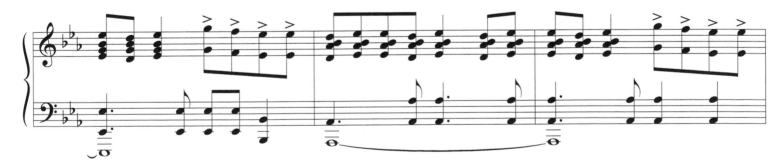

BEETHOVEN'S FIFTH

By Ludwig van Beethoven
Arranged by Jason Lyle Black

poco   a   poco   ac - cel - er -

an - do - - - - - - - - - - - - -

f   *ff*

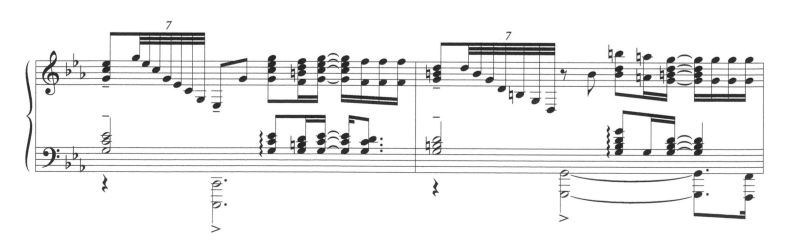

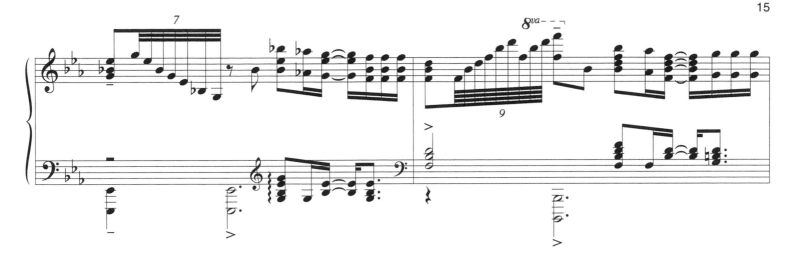

THE EVOLUTION OF TAYLOR SWIFT

Love Story • You Belong with Me • I Knew You Were Trouble • We Are Never Ever Getting Back Together
Shake It Off • Style • Blank Space • Bad Blood

Arranged by Jason Lyle Black

LOVE STORY
Words and Music by TAYLOR SWIFT

YOU BELONG WITH ME
Words and Music by TAYLOR SWIFT and LIZ ROSE

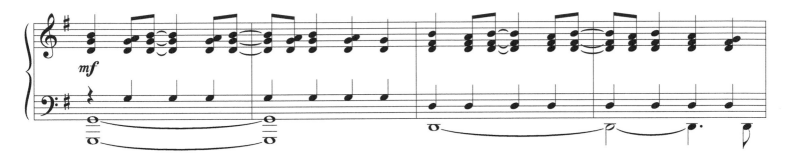

I KNEW YOU WERE TROUBLE
Words and Music by TAYLOR SWIFT, SHELLBACK and MAX MARTIN

WE ARE NEVER EVER GETTING BACK TOGETHER
Words and Music by TAYLOR SWIFT, SHELLBACK and MAX MARTIN

SHAKE IT OFF
Words and Music by TAYLOR SWIFT, MAX MARTIN and SHELLBACK

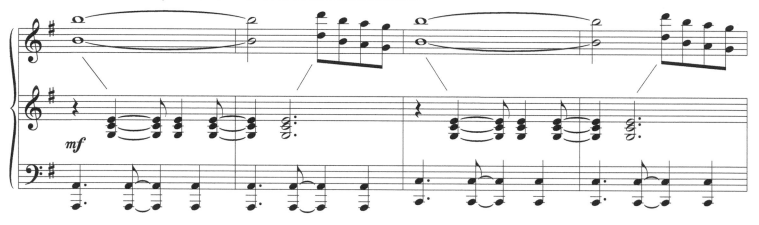

* To simplify this next section, play only the top notes in the R.H. instead of the octaves.

STYLE

Words and Music by TAYLOR SWIFT, MAX MARTIN, SHELLBACK and ALI PAYAMI

$\dot{\downarrow} = 90$

BLANK SPACE/BAD BLOOD

Words and Music by TAYLOR SWIFT, MAX MARTIN and SHELLBACK

$\dot{\downarrow} = 100$

STYLE

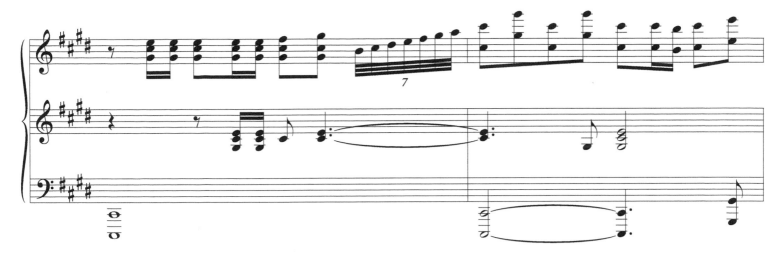

FROZEN MEDLEY

featuring songs from Disney's Animated Feature FROZEN

Love Is an Open Door • For the First Time in Forever • Do You Want to Build a Snowman? • Let It Go

Music and Lyrics by KRISTEN ANDERSON-LOPEZ
and ROBERT LOPEZ
Arranged by Jason Lyle Black

LOVE IS AN OPEN DOOR

FOR THE FIRST TIME IN FOREVER

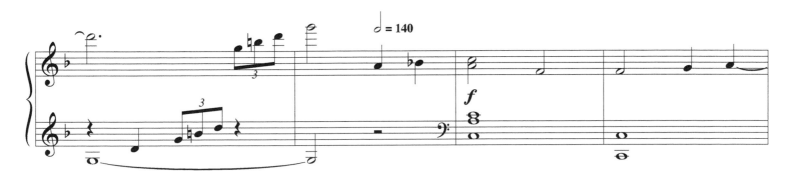

24

DO YOU WANT TO BUILD A SNOWMAN?

(click tongue)

LET IT GO

f

8vb

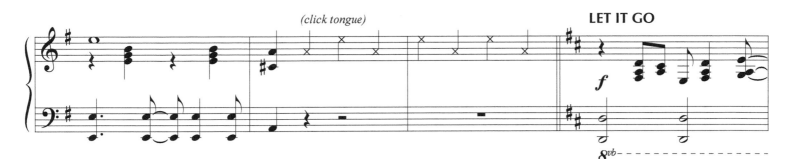

(8vb)

(8vb)

(8vb)

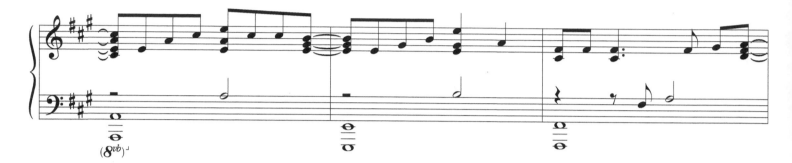

THE HANGING TREE

from the Original Motion Picture Soundtrack THE HUNGER GAMES: MOCKINGJAY – PART 1

Words and Music by SUZANNE COLLINS,
JEREMIAH FRAITES and WESLEY SCHULTZ
Arranged by Jason Lyle Black

I WILL WAIT

Words and Music by MUMFORD & SONS
Arranged by Jason Lyle Black

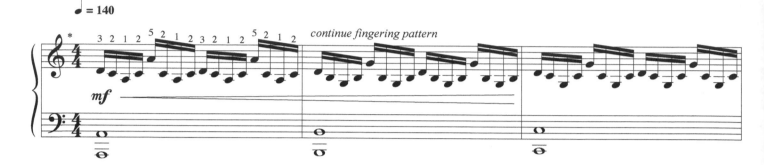

* *Originally recorded on YouTube in D♭ Major.*
Practice the sixteenth-note passages slowly and rotate your wrist as you play.

(8vb)

(suggested fingering)

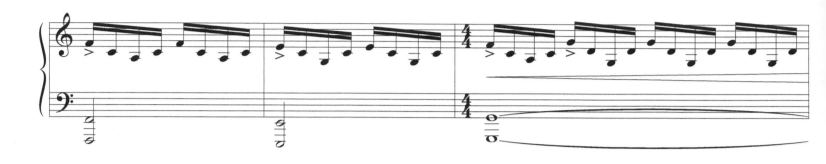

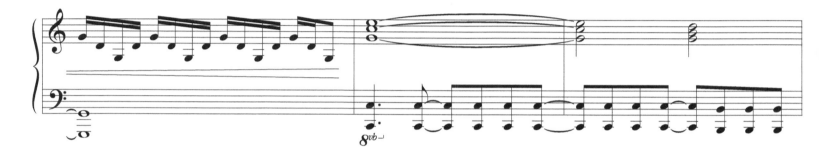

I WON'T GIVE UP
from the Motion Picture THE AVENGERS

Words and Music by JASON MRAZ
and MICHAEL NATTER
Arranged by Jason Lyle Black

RADIOACTIVE

Words and Music by DANIEL REYNOLDS,
BENJAMIN McKEE, DANIEL SERMON,
ALEXANDER GRANT and JOSH MOSSER
Arranged by Jason Lyle Black

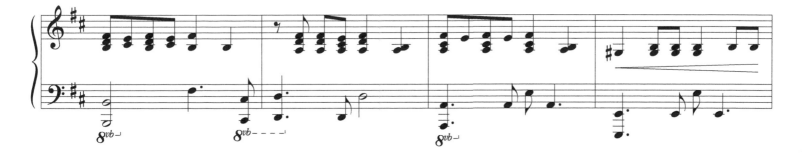

molto rit.

Much slower

p

ff

LIPS ARE MOVIN'

Words and Music by KEVIN KADISH
and MEGHAN TRAINOR
Arranged by Jason Lyle Black

SEE YOU AGAIN
from FURIOUS 7

Words and Music by CAMERON THOMAZ,
CHARLIE PUTH, JUSTIN FRANKS
and ANDREW CEDAR
Arranged by Jason Lyle Black

49

SHUT UP AND DANCE

Words and Music by RYAN McMAHON, BEN BERGER,
SEAN WAUGAMAN, ELI MAIMAN,
NICHOLAS PETRICCA and KEVIN RAY
Arranged by Jason Lyle Black

THRILLER

Words and Music by ROD TEMPERTON
Arranged by Jason Lyle Black

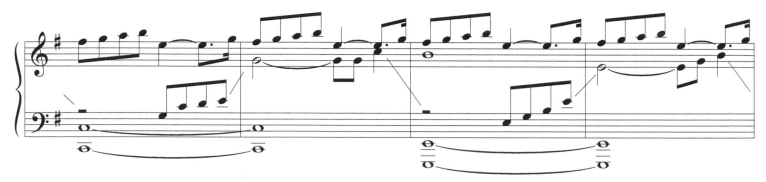

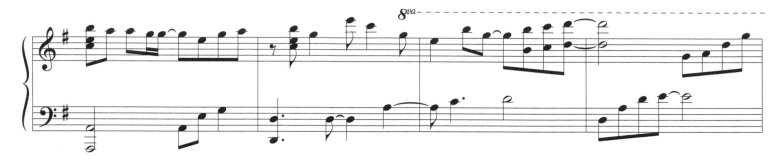

SUGAR

Words and Music by ADAM LEVINE, HENRY WALTER,
JOSHUA COLEMAN, LUKASZ GOTTWALD,
JACOB KASHER HINDLIN and MIKE POSNER
Arranged by Jason Lyle Black